Founding High Priest of the
Church of Satan

Anton LaVey Speaks

The Canonical Interview

JACK FRITSCHER

"This is the most candid and informative interview that Anton LaVey has given anyone for publication to date."
—Marcello Truzzi, *Fate* magazine

Palm Drive Publishing

Copyright © Jack Fritscher, 1970, 1972, 2004, and 2021.

Anton LaVey Speaks: The Canonical Interview © 1971, 1972, 2005, 2021 Jack Fritscher. All rights reserved. No part of this book may be used or reproduced in any manner whatsoever without written permission of the publisher, except in the case of brief quotations embodied in critical and academic works as well as reviews. For information, contact Palm Drive Publishing at www.PalmDrivePublishing.com.

The right of Jack Fritscher to be identified as author of this work has been asserted by him in accordance with the Copyright, Designs and Patents Act 1988.

Anton LaVey Speaks: The Canonical Interview was first published as part of Jack Fritscher's *Popular Witchcraft: Straight from the Witch's Mouth*, Bowling Green University Press, 1972.

Cover and book design by Mark Hemry

Published by Palm Drive Publishing, Sebastopol CA
www.PalmDrivePublishing.com
Email: publisher@PalmDrivePublishing.com

For author history and for historical research
www.JackFritscher.com

Fritscher, Jack, 1939–
Anton LaVey Speaks: The Canonical Interview / Jack Fritscher
p.cm.
ISBN 978-1-890834-56-2 Print
ISBN 978-1-890834-57-9 eBook

1. Witchcraft. I. LaVey Anton Szandor, 1930-1997. II. Title.

First Printing 2021
10 9 8 7 6 5 4 3 2
Palm Drive Publishing
www.PalmDrive Publishing.com

From the Canon of Witchcraft...

Foreword
Anton Szandor LaVey

**High Priest and Founder of the Church of Satan,
author of *The Satanic Bible*,
and Icon of 1960s Counter Culture
San Francisco, California
Midnight, July 29, 1971**

Anton Szandor LaVey invoked the United States Constitution on a night sacred to witches, *Walpurgisnacht*, April 30, 1966, when he founded his Church of Satan on the premise that Satanism is an ancient religion protected by the Constitution. On the next morning, May Day, the pagan feast of Beltane, his was a defining act during the cultural revolution of the 1960s. At 36, Anton LaVey was young enough to influence the best of the 60s, and old enough not to fall prey to the worst. He wrote his witchcraft manifesto, *The Satanic Bible*, that became an international bestseller. The media loved his invention of himself. The press named him the "Black Pope" and the "High Priest of the Church of Satan."

He appeared on magazine covers, and in San Francisco's strip of nightclubs in North Beach performing his "Topless Witches Sabbath." He played the role of His Satanic Majesty in gay director Kenneth Anger's 1969 film, *Invocation of My Demon Brother*, alongside Mick Jagger and future Manson Family killer Bobby Beausoleil. He told me in this interview that director Roman Polanski cast him as the Devil in *Rosemary's Baby*.

His controversial religion of Satanism was a human-interest lark to the hungry media for three years, until on the night of August 9, 1969, the Charles Manson Family killed Roman Polanski's pregnant movie-star wife, Sharon Tate, and several others, and changed everything in American popular culture concerning cult and coven, sex and violence. America demanded serious investigations. On the morning of August 10, 1969, the media anointed Anton LaVey as the point man to explain the dark side of American culture.

Anton LaVey became a lightning rod. He was feared, loved, hated, and respected. He became an icon of popular culture. He was called the "Devil Himself." Sprung from his intellect, and carried on his shoulders, the Church of Satan entered history, and will be mentioned for centuries to come.

Anton LaVey at six feet and 200 pounds certainly looked like the archetype of the archfiend: shaved head, goatee, piercing eyes, black clothes. When he invited me to his Victorian, the Black House, at 6114 California Street, San Francisco, he insisted I arrive at midnight as July 28 became Thursday, July 29, 1971. His companion, Diane Hegarty, to whom he dedicated *The Satanic Bible*, welcomed me into their parlor, invited me to have a seat in Rasputin's sleigh chair, and left me alone while the clock chimed twelve. The black room lined with book shelves resembled a faculty professor's home, except for the huge tombstone coffee table, the animal heads, the art and scarves and candles piercing the shimmering gloom.

To my left, the front parlor was painted black, with a red ceiling. Black curtains draped the windows through which I could not hear California Street. Against the west wall stood an altar installed over the fireplace. On its mantle, candles guttered. Shadows flickered on the wall above the altar where hung a huge painted baphomet of the traditional five-pointed star in a circle. Director Roger Corman has said that in a horror movie, a house is always a woman's body. This sanctuary perfectly reflected the centrality of women in the Church of Satan. In fact, Diane later joked that the altar was exactly sized to fit a woman, precisely her.

As the clock chimed fifteen minutes past midnight, a book case opposite the couch on which I was sitting, glided open. Anton LaVey appeared, all in black, wearing a Catholic priest's Roman collar and a red-lined Bela Lugosi cape. He was everything he was supposed to be. He was absolutely charming. He was every inch the assured embodiment of his proverb in *The Satanic Bible*: "Positive thinking and positive action add up to results." Our months of correspondence paid off. We each understood the other. For two and a half hours, we talked. Our time together was purposeful conversation as much as interview, even though, from start to finish, he watched me write notes on my yellow legal pad of every word he said.

At nearly three in the morning, Anton LaVey summoned Diane to join us. For thirty minutes, we three chatted. (It was then that Diane mentioned that the altar was perfect for a five-foot-three blonde woman, which, that being the message, she happened to be.) Anton LaVey asked me if I would like to participate in a ritual. But, of course. He asked Diane to bring out a baphomet amulet.

"I wish," he said, "to present you with this token." The three of us entered the front parlor. Diane stood to the side as a witness. Anton LaVey stood on the altar. I knelt on the altar step. I'm a journalist not a Satanist, but ritual to an ecumenical Catholic like me is universally familiar, and universally respected. Anton spoke his invocation, and raised the red-and-black enameled amulet, embossed with the pentagram and a goat face, hanging from a silver chain above my head. Again he made an invocation. I had been blessed by many priests, and he was blessing me again.

"Hail, Satan," he said.

"Hail, Satan," Diane said.

"Hail, Satan," I said.

The earth did not open up and swallow me. The ritual blessing was repeated three times. On the third solemn pass, Anton LaVey, High Priest of the Church of Satan, placed the silver chain over my head. The metal baphomet rested cold for a moment on my forehead. I felt his fingers pull at the chain which was a perfect circle with no clasp. I had never told him that in 1963 the Catholic Church had ordained me as an exorcist. As his fingers struggled to fit the chain over my head, the chain broke and the baphomet fell to the altar step and rolled across the floor.

Anton LaVey and I looked at each other.

It was one of those inquisitive moments when two people's eyes really connect.

In the way that women introduce irony to levitate seriousness, Diane said, "Oh, you're exactly like Anton. You have a big head."

We laughed.

We breathed.

We turned serious.

We hailed Satan one, twice, thrice more.

Then successfully, Anton LaVey, worked the chain down my head and across my face. My eyes studied up close the palms of his hands. He smelled human. Finally, the baphomet rested on my naked chest.

Since that time, Anton LaVey has told people how pleased he was with the way the interview I wrote turned out.

This seminal interview, conducted in the fifth Satanic Year, is the first and earliest in-depth interview given by Anton LaVey whose *Satanic Bible* had been published only sixteen months before in 1969. He was still rather reclusive because the Manson Family murders had threatened the public image of the Church of Satan. Villains like Manson, in olden days, were often the point of ignition for witch-burning. Anton LaVey personally had the "grace and gravitas" to help calm and correct American confusion.

Over the past fifty years, my interview of Anton LaVey has entered the classic Canon of Satanic Literature. Certainly, the candid conversation catches one of the most intriguing men of the 20th century around the moment when the Swinging 1960s became the Titanic 1970s. Here is the truth of what Anton LaVey said. He himself has frequently endorsed my accuracy. This is the restored Question and Answer version of my hand-written original.

My Midnight with Anton

Anton LaVey Speaks

Jack Fritscher: Aleister Crowley claimed he could summon the Devil to appear bodily in a room. Christians also believe in the physical presence of Satan. The New Testament is like "Starring Satan, Live, In Person." Like Jesus, Satan is incarnated. In their famous duel, Satan tempts Jesus to fall down and worship his Satanic body.

Anton LaVey: I don't feel that raising the Devil in an anthropomorphic sense is quite as feasible as theologians or metaphysicians would like to think. I have felt his presence but only as an exteriorized extension of my own potential, as an alter-ego or evolved concept that I have been able to exteriorize. With a full awareness, I can communicate with this semblance, this creature, this Demon, this personification that I see in the eyes of the symbol of Satan–the Goat of Mendes–as I commune with him before the altar. None of these is anything more than a mirror image of that potential I perceive in myself.

Fritscher: Like the Beatles' "I am he and you are me and we are all together." Is the self Satan?

LaVey: I have this awareness that the objectification is in accord with my own ego. I'm not deluding myself that I'm calling something that is disassociated or exteriorized from myself the Godhead. This Force is not a controlling factor that I have no control over. The Satanic principle is that man willfully controls his destiny.

Fritscher: The triumph of the will. So a person controls what's internal to control the external?

LaVey: If he doesn't, some other man—a lot smarter than he is—will. Satan is, therefore, an extension of one's psyche or volitional essence, so that the extension can sometimes converse and give directives through the self in a way that mere thinking of the self as a single unit cannot. In this way it *does* help to depict in an externalized way the Devil *per se.* The purpose is to have something of an idolatrous, objective nature to commune with. However, man has connection, contact, control. This notion of an exteriorized God-Satan is not new.

Fritscher: Idolatry. God and Satan projected out of our own psyches...

LaVey: Our sexual psyches. For instance, my opinion of the succubus and incubus is that these are dream manifestations of man's coping with guilt, as in the case of nocturnal emissions with a succubus visiting a man or of erotic dreams with an incubus visiting a woman. This whole idea of casting the blame off one's own sexual feelings onto convenient Demons to satisfy the Church has certainly proved useful in millions of cases.

Fritscher: Bless me, Father, for I have sinned, but "The Devil made me do it."

LaVey: That's exactly the scene when the priest is confronted one morning by a parishioner holding a stiffened nightshirt, a semen-encrusted nightgown. The priest can tell him about this "terrible" succubus who visited him in the night. They proceed to exorcise the Demon, getting the parishioner off the sexual hook and giving the priest a little prurient fun as he plays with the details of its predication on some pretty girl in the village. This, on top of it all, leaves the girl suspect of being a witch.

Fritscher: When all else fails, blame the woman.

LaVey: Naturally the priest can keep his eyes open. He has the power to decide who fits the succubus descriptions that he's heard in the confessional. Of course, the concept of incubi and succubi has also been used by people who have engaged in what they would consider illicit sexual relations. More than one lady's window has been left open purposely for the incubus to enter–in the form of some desirable male. They can both then chalk it up the next day to Demonic possession. All these very convenient dodges have kept Christianity and its foibles alive for many hundreds of years.

Fritscher: You mean, I think, that sex has kept Christianity in business. When I look at Satanism, I see Christianity reversed. What Christianity does with the right hand, Satanism does with the left. Like Christ and Anti-Christ.

LaVey: The birth of a Satanic child is another manifestation of the need to extend the Christ-myth of the virgin birth to an antithetical concept of a Demonic birth, a Devil-child. *Rosemary's Baby* wasn't the first to use this age-old plot. The Devil's own dear son or daughter is a rather popular literary excursion. Certainly the Devil walks in the sinews and marrow of a man because the Devil is the representation of fleshly deity. Any animal heritage, any natural predilections, any real human attributes would be seen as the personification of the Devil.

Fritscher: Precisely the philosophy of Protestant Puritanism and Catholic Jansenism. Humans are essentially depraved, evil animals.

LaVey: And the Devil is proud of them. Just as the Devil would have offspring and be proud of them, antithetic as they are to Christianity. Christians are ashamed that the child was conceived in sin and baptized out of sin. The Devil revels in the lust-conception of his child. This child would be involved much more magically than one who was the by-product of an environment that sought to negate at first opportunity the very motivating force—the carnal desire—that produced him.

Fritscher: So when baptism washes away original sin, it also washes away magic and sex.

LaVey: Yes. And not just Christianity. Religion itself demeans our carnal nature. Religious artists' desexualizing of the birth process—picturing Christ coming out of the bowels of Mary—has caused women to suffer childbirth pains much more than they need to because of the age-old collective unconsciousness that women must suffer this and the periodic suffering that comes every 28 days. Both these are attempts to stamp out or discredit what are in the animal world the most passionate female feelings when the animal comes into heat at that time of the month. The "curse" of the menstrual cycle is a manufactured thing, manufactured by society that recognizes this period as one of great desire. Automatically, we have overemphasized its pains, tensions, turmoil, cramps. This taboo is not just Christian. Women have been placed in huts outside many villages. Every culture has thought women would cause more jealousy and turmoil at this time because of this increase in her passions. Male animals fight more when the female is in heat. Having been a lion tamer, I know even the females are more combative at this time.

Christianity has subjected modern women to even more self-recrimination. This is the big difference between tribal customs and Christian. In the tribe, the woman is considered to be bleeding poison. In Christianity the woman is not only considered taboo, but she has to endure her pain as a "moral" reminder of her mortality and guilt. The primitive woman can give birth relatively painlessly and return to the fields. She goes through the physical act, but not through the moral agonies of the Christian woman. Such is the compounding of guilt. This kind of hypocrisy is my "Enemy Number One."

Fritscher: That's why the establishment fears you. Your voice adds to the counter-culture revolution.

LaVey: Out there in the streets, I don't think young people can be blamed too much for their actions and antics. Although they coat their protests in ideological issues, I think what they resent most is not the actions of older adults, but the gross hypocrisy under which adults act. What is far worse than making war is making war and calling it *peace* and *love* and saying it's "waged under the auspices of God" or that "it's the Christian thing to do." Onward, Christian soldiers and all that! I think that the worst thing about Christianity is its gross hypocrisy which is the most repugnant thing in the world to me. Most Christians practice a basic Satanic...

Fritscher: Satanic?

LaVey: ...Satanic way of life every hour of their waking day and yet they sneer at somebody who has built a religion that is no different from what they're practicing, but is simply calling it by its right name. I call it by the name that is antithetical to that which they hypocritically pay lip-service when they're in church.

Fritscher: They burn people like you at the stake.

LaVey: Precisely. Take, for example, the roster of people executed for witchcraft in the Middle Ages. They were unjustly maligned because they were free-thinkers, beautiful girls, heretics, Jews...

Fritscher: Homosexuals...

LaVey: And lesbians, or people who happened to be of a different faith than was ordained. They were mercilessly tortured and exterminated without any thought of Christian charity. The basic lies and propaganda of the Christian Fathers added to the torment of the people. Yet the crime in today's streets and the mollycoddling of heinous criminals is a by-product of latter-day Christian charity. Christian "understanding" has made our city streets unsafe. Yet helpless millions of people, simply because they were unbelievers or disbelievers, were not "understood." They were killed. It's not right that a mad dog who is really dangerous should be "understood" and those who merely dissent from Christianity should have been killed. At the Church of Satan we receive lots of damning letters from people condemning us in the most atrocious language. They attest they are good Christians, but they are full of hate. They don't know if I'm a good guy or a bad guy. They only know me by the label they've been taught: that Satanism is evil. Therefore they judge me on the same basis those people did in the 13th through 16th centuries.

Fritscher: The Inquisition has never stopped.

LaVey: These very same people hardly ever get worked up over a murderer.

Fritscher: They fear that your Satan debunks their Jesus.

LaVey: They fear. I think. Christ has failed in all his engagements as both savior and deity. If his doctrines were that easily misinterpreted, if his logic was that specious, let's throw it out. It has no place. It is worthless to a civilized society if it is subject to gross misinterpretation. I'm not just protesting the "human element'" in Christianity the way Christians do when something goes wrong with their system. I void the whole of the system that lends itself to such misinterpretation.

Fritscher: Protestantism made Catholicism worse. Rome dictated exactly what the Bible meant. Protestants reacted and opened the Bible up to the chaos of private interpretation.

LaVey: Why the hell didn't the writers mean what they said or say what they meant when they wrote that stupid book of fables, the Bible? This is the way I feel about it.

Fritscher: How do you feel, then, about Wicca, or white magic? Pagans I've talked with feel robbed because early Christianity sucked up their beliefs and rites the way the Church turned the Roman Empire into the Holy Roman

Empire which turned into the Vatican that rules more people than Caesar ever conquered.

LaVey: Anybody who takes up the sanctimonious "cult of white light" is just playing footsy with the Christian Fathers. This is why the bane of my existence are these white witches, white magicians, people who'd like to keep their foot in the safety zone of righteousness. They refuse to see the Demonic in themselves, the motivations Satan's Majesty and Nature have placed inside them for their terrestrial goal. Materialism is part of Satanism, but a right kind of materialism. Everyone wants to acquire. The only thing wrong with money is it falls into the wrong hands. This makes it a curse, a disadvantage rather than an advantage. The marketplace is full of thieves. Easy wealth may be something would-be Faustian Satanists would like to get hold of.

Fritscher: You can "make things happen"? Certain things that people want? Practical magic?

LaVey: In my experience, people have come to me after I had opened doors for them. They got what they wanted. Very quickly, they come back wanting to know how to turn "it" off as they have more troubles than they had before. Once I offer to people what they think they want, given a week to think it over, they get cold feet.

Fritscher: Ah. You are saying, like Saint Thérèse of Lisieux and Truman Capote, that there's more tears shed over answered prayers...

LaVey: Success is a threat. Threatened by success, most people show their true colors. They show they need a God or an astrological forecast to really lay the blame on for their own inadequacy in the threatening face of imminent success.

Fritscher: Your basic tenet: everything is personal, rooted in the person.

LaVey: Man needs religion, dogma, ritual that keeps him exteriorized outside of himself to waylay his guilt and inadequacy. Men will always, therefore, search for a God. We should, however, be men in search of man.

Fritscher: Satanism is the ultimate humanism.

LaVey: That at least makes sense I can see, hear, and touch. The man in search of God is the masochist. He is the world's masochist. There are more than we imagine.

Fritscher: Religion attracts masochistic exhibitionists who like to suffer public penances and denial of the flesh. It's common.

LaVey: In the beginning, I may not have intended Satanism to evolve into an elitist movement. But experience has taught me that Satanism can be a mass movement only insofar as its basic pleasure-seeking premise is concerned.

Fritscher: Attached to sexual freedom.

LaVey: You build a better mousetrap, and people are going to flock to it. A pleasure principle is going to be more popular than denying pleasure. I can't help attracting the masses. As for the people who practice a truly Satanic way of life, you can't expect the masses to transcend mere lip-service to the pleasure-seeking principle and get into the magical state of the Absolute Satanist.

Fritscher: Is the Absolute Satanist transcendent? Self-reliant? Self-creating?

LaVey: The Absolute Satanist is totally aware of his own abilities and limitations. On this self-knowledge he builds his character. The Absolute Satanist is far removed from the masses who look for Satanic pleasure in the psychedelics of the head shops. We Satanists are magically a part of all this surface culture. I realize what my magical lessons have done, the things I've stumbled upon. We necessarily spawn our neo-Christian masses seeking their sense of *soma* through pills and drugs. Certainly I don't oppose this for other people who get stoned out of their minds. When they do this, the more material things there will be for me and my followers since all those people who freaked themselves out on drugs will be satisfied with their pills and will move off to colonies based on drugs. The rest of us, the Materialists, will inherit the world.

Fritscher: So Absolute Satanism is humanism and materialism. But is Satanism narcissism? Drugs, which you have always denounced, are very narcissistic.

LaVey: Actually, I'm very much opposed to drugs from a magical point of view, from a *control* point of view. I feel drugs are antithetical to magic. The pseudo-Satanist or pseudo-witch or self-styled mystic who predicates his success on a drug revelation is only going to succeed within his drugged peer group. His miracles go no farther than his credibility. This type of witchery is limited. This, I say, despite the fact that the druggies are no longer just a marginal group, but are a very large subculture which threatens to be the "New Spirituality" or the "New Mysticism" or the "New Non-Materialism."

Fritscher: So the drug culture, despite its visions on peyote and acid, is narcissistic in that it turns in on itself and accomplishes nothing. Witchcraft, on the other hand, is a means to an end.

LaVey: The whole concept of witchery is manipulation of other human beings, as means to the end you want.

Fritscher: You give an essential definition, and clear motivation.

LaVey: Druggies don't realize that. Druggies are not manipulative witches. To manipulate someone you've got to be able to relate to that someone. Their idea of witchery is not witchcraft so much–in the sense of witchery being manipulative magic–as witchery equaling revelation of a spiritual nature.

Fritscher: Two different goals. Power and mysticism.

LaVey: Their superego gets developed through the use of drugs. This superego can be the ear-mark of a new world of drones who, through *soma*, would attain superegos which allow them while so controlled to think they have superiority over those really enjoying the fruits of the earth. This is why as the leader of the Satanic movement I have to examine these popular movements in the culture from a very pragmatic point of view.

Fritscher: Which is why I thank you for us sitting together tonight. You and the Church of Satan are perfectly relevant to the study of popular culture.

LaVey: The point is there will always be, among the masses, substitutes for the real thing. A planned way of life–not drugs–gets the materialist what he wants. There's nothing wrong with color TV and cars in the garage as long as the system which provides them respects "law and order"–a terribly overworked term.

But as long as people don't bother other people, then I think this is an ideal society.

I'm in favor of a policeman on every corner–as long as he doesn't arrest people for thinking their own way, or for doing within the privacy of their own four walls what they like to do.

Fritscher: You are speaking, are you not, of your operating your Church of Satan? Which is, of course, the freedom to practice your religion. You are wise to have chosen San Francisco which has always been an open city.

LaVey: We haven't been hassled too much by the law because we have so many policemen in our organization. I'm an ex-cop myself. I worked in the crime lab in San Francisco and I've maintained my contacts. They've provided for me a kind of security force. But all in all we have a very clean slate. [He laughs.] We are very evil outlaws in theological circles, but not in civil.

How could we murder? We–unlike Christians–have a real regard for human bodies.

The Satanist is the ultimate humanist.

The Satanist realizes that man can be his own worst enemy and must often be protected against himself. The average man sets up situations for himself so he can be a loser. We Satanists have ancient rituals which exorcise those needs for self-abasement before they happen. We wreck Christians' tidy little dreams.

When you have a born-again Christian rolling orgasmically on the floor at a revival meeting claiming an ecstasy, you tell them they're having a "forbidden" orgasm and they hate you for enlightening them. You've robbed them of their "succubus"...

Fritscher: You're so evil, you're good.

LaVey: ...of their freedom from guilt. They push their evilness on to us. In this sense, then, we are *very* evil.

Fritscher: How does the public person you are impact your private life? Americans know you baptized your daughter into the Church of Satan. Does she go to school with Rosemary's baby?

LaVey: I needn't send my child to a private school. Why should I, when children are, in fact, all natural Satanists, perfect at manipulating everyone.

Fritscher: Undoubtedly, she will be a perfect heir.

LaVey: My daughter has no trouble at school. The majority of our members are from the middle-class. At least fifty percent of our members have children. But our members do not proselytize at their children's schools. Our members rarely discuss sex, religion, and politics with outsiders.

Fritscher: What about your own politics? What about law and order and civil rights?

LaVey: I was very liberal in my younger years. I would have been thrown into prison during the McCarthy purge [1951-1952] had I been of any prominence.

Fritscher: You would not have cooperated with the government.

LaVey: I was ultra-liberal, attending meetings of the Veterans of the Spanish Civil War, the Abraham Lincoln Brigade, the Revisionist Movements of Israel's founding. This was all very liberal at the time. I was always for civil rights. I had Negro friends when Negro friends weren't fashionable. A man should be judged on his accomplishments, his kindness and consideration for others. A certain planned form of bigotry may be a little healthy. I mean, if a person is the worst that his race has produced, he should be prevented from using his race as a means to make his way unless he is a credit to his race, religion, whatever it is.

Fritscher: You mean revolutionaries like Huey Newton? Eldridge Cleaver? The Black Panthers?

LaVey: Martin Luther King was killed because he was an articulate gentleman, concerned about his wife and family. He tried to do things in a mannerly way. A man like that belongs on a pedestal. But these loud baboons–and I choose the term–are nothing but rabble rousers, spewing venom. The more a person has at stake the more he watches his *p's* and *q's*. This is my test of a person's sincerity. The public is no judge. The public is not too particular in its choosing of heroes.

Fritscher: Yours is a powerful voice saying things that scare people who fear what they don't understand.

LaVey: I voted for George Wallace to act out a magical ritual.[1] I performed the political ritual–knowing Wallace would not win, but wishing simply to cast my runes. Wallace's advantage was he would have been helpful in the inert area between *action* and *reaction*. The pendulum is swinging.

---

1 Wallace, segregationist governor of Alabama, ran for president of the United States on a third-party ticket in 1968 causing the defection of southern Democrats from the Democratic Party, which thus made possible the election of Republican Richard Nixon who was forced to resign the presidency for his political crimes. The Green Party's Ralph Nader repeated this political ritual in 2000 making possible the presidency of George W. Bush who said that witchcraft is not a religion.

I've been misinterpreted when I've said people like Reagan and Nixon are doing a lot to help Satanism because they are causing tremendous popular reaction–whereby we're getting off the hook in Vietnam.

Fritscher: Racial anarchy, war, social chaos, women's lib. Your opinions are interesting in these first years of your Church of Satan, insofar, as right now you *are* the Church of Satan. You have many opinions. Are they subject to change?

LaVey: Even the Church of Satan will change as time goes by.

Fritscher: What do you make of these changing times? Of popular culture versus the government?

LaVey: Popular opinion is simply a reaction against the leaders who have made their stand so heinous that the protestors don't realize they're doing exactly what the masters want them to do: they're getting the masters off the hook. The masters are using the old magical technique of manipulating the people to think it's their idea to end the war.

Fritscher: So the government is using magic, or is it just reverse psychology?

LaVey: Same manipulation. This explains the government's permissive attitude toward protest. The idealists of the early 50s during the McCarthy era were certainly just as against war; but the government then wanted a posture of cold war. So they had to be shut up fast. Currently the show of rebellion is a very magical ritual approved by the government which is trying to direct the inevitability of change.

Fritscher: Some say this is a magic time, because revolution, change, is upon us. Change is the essence of magic, of changing one thing into another, of tricksters shifting shapes. American parents think their hippie children are changeling babies.

LaVey: In the change that is coming the new emphasis will be placed on staging. Life is a game and we'll realize it's a game. Life is not "God's Will."

Fritscher: Is it "Satan's Will"?

LaVey: Whose will is Satan's Will? We have to go to the point of no return before we can return. We will get to the point where anybody who is establishment-oriented is suspect as being the worst kind of individual. This will happen before we return to a rather safe normality, to a sane discrimination as to who are really the contributing members of society and who are the cancerous tissue.

Satanically speaking, anarchy and chaos must ensue for awhile before a new Satanic morality can prevail. The new Satanic morality won't be very different from the old law of the jungle wherein right and wrong were judged in the truest natural sense of biting and being bitten back. Satanic morality will cause a return to intrigue, to glamour, to seductiveness, to a modicum of sexual lasciviousness. Taboos will be invoked, but mostly it will be realized these things are fun.

Fritscher: Fun already is the heart of movements like the hippies and gay lib, and maybe women's lib.

LaVey: The various liberation fronts are all part of the omelet from which the New Satanic Morality will emerge. Women's Liberation is really quite humorous. Supposedly women were liberated after the Industrial Revolution when they got out of the sweatshops. Women are going to defeat themselves, because they're not using the ammunition of their femininity to win as women. They're trying to reject their femininity which is their greatest magical weapon.

Fritscher: This I know. *The Satanic Bible* tells me so.

LaVey: Women are parodying themselves.

Fritscher: Some people will not want to hear that.

LaVey: Speaking of parody, Christians will not want to hear this. The historical Black Mass is a parody of a parody.

Fritscher: You mean the Black Mass where the woman is the altar, and sex and sacrilege are committed on her body to defy Christ...the way the French revolutionaries did on the altar of Notre Dame.

LaVey: Making fun of the Catholic Mass, yes. The Black Mass parodies the Christian service which parodies a pagan. Every time a man and woman go to church on Sunday they are practicing a Black Mass by parodying "ancient earth rituals" which were practiced by their ancestors before they were *inverted* by the Christian Fathers.

Fritscher: Not converted?

LaVey: Inverted. Our Satanic Mass is not a parody of the Catholic Mass. Our Satanic Mass celebrates the power of the self, the beauty of the self. We ritualize that. Our Mass is catharsis. The Women's Lib-ists, for the same kind of catharis, should simply use their femininity by taking the Devil's name and playing the Devil's game. They should take the stigma that cultural guilt has thrown at women and invert the values. Just as words have power, the semantic reversal of those words is also powerful.

Fritscher: So if someone calls a woman a witch, or worse, she should co-opt the epithet and turn it into a compliment. Change a bad word into good?

LaVey: This is the essence of what we have done in Satanism. What theologians have supplied in stigma, we change to virtue. We therefore have the attraction of the forbidden. This has greatly aided our success.

Fritscher: On the subject of women, how exactly was Jayne Mansfield connected to the Church of Satan?

LaVey: I know I have been rumored to have cursed Jayne Mansfield and caused her death. [Buxom blonde movie star Mansfield, alleged lover of President John Kennedy, was decapitated in a car crash driving out of New Orleans on the foggy night of June 29, 1967.] Jayne Mansfield was a member of the Church of Satan. I have enough material to blow sky-high all those sanctimonious Hollywood journalists who claim she wasn't. She was a priestess in the Church of Satan. I have documentation of this fact from her. There are many things I'll not say for obvious reasons.

Fritscher: Say what you can.

LaVey: Her lover [lawyer, Sam Brody, also killed in the front seat of the car], who was a decidedly unsavory character, was the one who brought the curse upon himself. There was decidedly a curse, marked in the presence of other people. Jayne was warned constantly and periodically in no uncertain terms that she must avoid his company because great harm would befall him. It was a very sad sequence of events in which she was the victim of her own–as we mentioned earlier–inability to cope with her own success. Also the "Demonic Self" in her was crying out to be one thing, and her "Apparent Self" demanded that she be something else. She was beaten back and forth in this inner conflict between the "Apparent Self" and the "Demonic Self." Sam Brody was blackmailing her.

Fritscher: About what?

LaVey: He was blackmailing her. I have definite proof of this. She couldn't get out of his clutches. She was a bit of a masochist herself. She brought about her own demise. But it wasn't through what I had done to curse *her*. The curse, that she asked me to cast, was directed at *him*. And it was a very magnificent curse.

Fritscher: Your *Satanic Bible* is dedicated to a pop culture pantheon from Rasputin and Ragnar Redbeard to a bevy of Hollywood blondes.

LaVey: The dedication of my *Satanic Bible* to Jayne Mansfield, Marilyn Monroe, and Tuesday Weld [the blonde movie star of *Lord Love a Duck*, *Pretty Poison*, *Play It As It Lays*, and *Who'll Stop the Rain*] was, in Marilyn's case, homage to a woman who was literally victimized by her own inherent witchery potential which was there in her looks. I think a great deal of the female mystique of beauty which was personified in Marilyn's image. In the case of Tuesday Weld, it's part of the magical ritual. She is my candidate of a living approximation of these other two women. Unlike them, Tuesday has the intelligence and emotional stability to withstand that which Marilyn Monroe could not. For this reason Tuesday is not in the public eye as much. Her own better judgment has cautioned her not to bite off more than she can chew.

Fritscher: The way you reference history you are very successful at reminding America how deeply ingrained Satanism is in society from colonial times to the present.

LaVey: History is character. Modern Puritans need to know that the popular American hero, Ben Franklin, was a rake without question. He was a sensual dilettante. He joined up with the British Hellfire Club. Their rituals came to them from the Templars and other secret societies. We practice some of these same rituals secretly in the Church of Satan. Not only did Ben Franklin influence the activities of the Hellfire Club, his very association sheds some light on the *quality* of members of what would appear to be a blasphemous group of individuals. This proves the Devil is not only a gentleman, but a cultured gentleman.

Fritscher: Pop culture brags that we live in an age of "Beautiful People." You like blonde women. What about physical beauty, or the lack of it? Thomas Aquinas says grace builds on nature. What does Satanic grace build on?

LaVey: Beauty, yes. And the eye of the beholder. Throughout history, the witch most feared is the witch most antithetical to the physical standards of beauty. In Mediterranean cultures, anyone with blue eyes would have been the first to be named as a witch. The Black woman, Tituba, in Salem was antithetical to New England physical standards or race. Anyone who is dark has an edge because of all the connotations of black arts, black magic, the dark and sinister side of human nature. Tituba probably was not only more feared but also more sought after. She was set apart physically from the rest of the people. She was the magical outsider.

Fritscher: Homosexuals are outsiders. Does a queer stand a chance in hell?

LaVey: In terms of homosexuality, the Church of Satan does not invite males as altars simply because the male is not considered to be the receptacle or passive carrier of human life. He possesses the other half of what is necessary to produce life. Woman is focal as receiver of the seed in her recumbent role as absorbing altar. A male would defeat the purpose of receptor unless he were fitted out with an artificial vagina and were physically and biologically capable of symbolizing the Earth Mother.

Fritscher: So you conjure on the basic heterosexual act. Yet, alternatively, Aleister Crowley used male sodomy to conjure Satan, and the white magician, Alex Sanders, used mutual male masturbation to create a spirit guide.

LaVey: They're British, aren't they. [Laughs] We do, however, accept homosexuals. We have many in the Church of Satan. They have to be well-adjusted homosexuals–and there *are* many well-adjusted homosexuals who are not on the daily defensive about their sexual persuasion. Many have a great amount of self-realization. Of course, we get the cream of the crop. Because, however, homosexuals cannot relate to the basic heterosexuality of the Church of Satan, whatever they do must be modified. Care would have to be taken, because if the homophile were involved in defining the dogma of our Church, it could become very imbalanced for the masses of people with whom we deal. The homosexual would very easily like to substitute a male for the female altar.

Fritscher: Many Catholic priests are homosexual, as are many Protestant ministers, as are many white witches.

LaVey: And most heterosexual congregations don't mind, because it's a fact that a heterosexual can accept homosexuality more readily than a homosexual can accept heterosexuality. Relating to the existence of the opposite sex is something that *must* be in evidence. Women cannot be denied their function in our Satanic Church. Needless to add, man-hating women cause us a great lack of, shall we say, sensual scintillation.

My book *The Complete Witch; or What to Do When Virtue Fails* is a guide for witches. It doesn't stress the drawing of pentacles on the floor. It smashes all the misconceptions that women have had, not only about witchery, but about their own sexuality. I think of this book like Simone de Beauvoir's *The Second Sex*. Even if a woman is a man-hater, she can use her femininity to ruin that man. This book tells her how to do it. If she wants to enjoy men, this book will open her eyes to a few things about her power.

Fritscher: Fetishes are important in magic, but what about sexual fetishes in the Church of Satan?

LaVey: Sexual fetishes we find natural. Everybody has one. These should be catered to. Sexual deviations are only negative factors when they present an obstacle to one's success. They present an obstacle when they are carried out of the ritual chamber, out of the fantasy room into the world where others will see them disapprovingly.

Fritscher: So homosexuals and sexual fetishists can belong to a Satanic coven as long as their impulses do not impede ritual or self-realization.

LaVey: As long as the men pursue their male power, and the women their female power, and they do not try to apply their sex power to manipulate others of the same gender. Self realization, more than the sex act, is the main tenet of Satanism.

Fritscher: You mean the way Rosemary realized by the end of *Rosemary's Baby* who she was, and accepted her child.

LaVey: I must tell you something quite amusing. *Rosemary's Baby* did for us what *Birth of a Nation* did for the Ku Klux Klan. The first Satanic Year was 1966. *Rosemary's Baby* premiered in 1968. I never realized what that film could do. I remember reading that at the premiere of D. W. Griffith's *Birth of a Nation* [Hollywood epic, 1915] there were recruiting posters for the KKK in southern cities. I chuckled because at the premiere of *Rosemary's Baby,* there were posters of the Church of Satan in the lobby. Here at the San Francisco premiere there was a great deal of consternation, but the film started an influx of very worthwhile new members. Since *Rosemary,* the quality of membership has gone up. Immeasurably.

Since that film with Roman Polanski, I am constantly confronted with scripts by thick-skulled exploitation producers who want me either to be technical advisor or play the role of the Devil or the Satanic doctor in their new films. They think to one-up *Rosemary*. What they don't realize is that *Rosemary's Baby* was popularly successful because it exploded a lot of the preconceptions of Satanism. It didn't chop up the baby at the end. Rosemary took her baby to her breast exactly like Christianity's Virgin Mary. It threw all the crap down the drain and showed the public who was expecting the sensational the real image of the Satanist. It will remain a masterpiece.

Fritscher: Hollywood pop culture explains Satanism.

LaVey: *Rosemary's Baby*, of course, was the allegory of the Christ Child told in reverse. The baby represented the Birth of the New Satanic Age, 1966. The year 1966 was used in *Rosemary's Baby*, as the date of the baby's birth, because 1966 was our Satanic Year One in the Church of Satan. The birth of the baby was the birth of Satanism. *Rosemary's Baby* stands foursquare against the popular image of child sacrifice. The role that I played in the picture–the Devil in the shaggy suit–was not from my point of view anything other than it should have been. I was man, animal, bestial, carnal nature coming forth in a ritualized way. The impregnation of Rosemary in that dream sequence was to me the very essence of the immodest, the bestial in man, impregnating the virginal world-mind with the re-awakening of the animalism within oneself. This impregnation was very meaningful because it showed the spawning literally, in the movie, of the Church of Satan. Among all the rituals in the film, this was the big ritual in *Rosemary's Baby*.

These other movie-makers who want my opinion on their scripts are simply producing more trash of the blood-sacrifice variety. In *Rosemary's Baby*, the girl who went out the window and landed on the pavement died in the pure Satanic tradition. She had made it clear—although the people who saw the film didn't realize it—that she was a loser. Everything she said pointed to it. She'd been kicked around. She'd been on the streets. She'd been on dope. She was obviously the wrong girl to be a carrier. Satan saw her lack of maternal instinct, of winning instinct, of spunk to carry this baby out into the world. She, therefore, sort of fell "accidentally" out the window. The end of the film shows Rosemary throw away her Catholic heritage and cherish the Devil-Child. The natural instinct of Satanism wins out in her woman's heart over man-made programming.

Fritscher: Rosemary wins.

LaVey: Rosemary is a triumphant woman, because she reaches self-realization.

Fritscher: Satan wins in your parallel to Christianity. Most movies have a traditional moral ending where good triumphs. You and Polanski are announcing a new ending.

LaVey: Even though I have done the consulting for *Mephisto Waltz* for 20th-Century-Fox, that film still has the old elements of witchery.

Fritscher: More old cliches rather than modern blasphemy?

LaVey: It's going to take a lot to come up with a film that's as much a blasphemy as *Rosemary's Baby*. Polanski's other film, *The Fearless Vampire Killers*, is like nothing else that's ever been done before in the film world. That film explodes all the puerile Christian myths about vampires. The old professor, sort of a Count Dracula, is shown to be not only the doddering old fool he really is, but also the real victim at the end. There's more to real Satanism than that.

Fritscher: You mean Satanists now resist the Inquisition.

LaVey: We'll never be victims again. Satanism is self-realization. Self-realization is power.

Fritscher: As the Black Pope, you must protect yourself, your family, your Church. How do you cope with the tragedy that befell Roman Polanski when his wife, his unborn baby, and his wife's guests were butchered by the Manson Family?

LaVey: The fact that all those unfortunate murders took place at Polanski's home–his wife Sharon Tate and all the rest–was used by the press to highlight Polanski's interest in witchery and Satanism. The deaths had nothing to do with the films. The Polanski household was simply plagued with hippies and drug addicts. If I were to allow it, my house would be full of sycophantic loungers.

Fritscher: You are like a rock star.

LaVey: I was in show biz. I know. If I allowed hangers-on, if I neglected them, they'd be paranoid. I would have been put in the same position as those people at Polanski's house had I allowed it. Polanski attracted, as people in Hollywood do, all the creeps, kooks, and crackpots. He wasn't around to stop it, or was too nice to put his foot down. He, in a sense, put himself in much the same position as Jayne Mansfield.[2]

---

[2] Roman Polanski won the Academy Award as Best Director for *The Pianist*, but he could not be present at the March 23, 2003, Oscar telecast in Hollywood as he remained a fugitive from America because of his conviction for statutory rape with a 13-year-old girl in 1979.

Those people that were killed at Polanski's house were all freaked out of their minds anyway. They were people who were only a little better than the killers. As far as their warped outlooks on life, their senses of values, it was a case of the blind destroying the blind. Sharon was probably the victim of her environment, but I can't find it in myself to whitewash these murdered people. I know first-hand how the people at Warhol's Factory and the Daisy discotheque and these other nightclubs behave. They're quite indiscriminate as to the people they take up with.

Fritscher: If anyone knows, you do. What *does* the Devil look like?

LaVey: The Devil in *Rosemary's Baby* was depicted as a combination of many anthropomorphic ideals of the bestial man: the reptilian scales, the fur, claws. A combination of the animal kingdom. It was not a red union-suit with a pitchfork. Nor was it Pan transmogrified by Christians into a cloven-hoofed Devil. *The Cloven Hoof* title of our newsletter was chosen precisely for its eclectic image in the popular mind as one of the Devil's more familiar and acceptable traits. Cloven-hoofed animals in pre-Christian times had often been considered sacred in their association with carnal desire. The pig, goat, ram–all of these creatures–are consistently associated with the Devil. Hence our title.

The truest concept of Satan is not in any one animal, but is in man, the evolutionary epitome of all animals. That's what Satan looks like.

Fritscher: Catholicism teaches that hell is hot; witchcraft says that Satan's penis is cold.

LaVey: The historical notion that Satan has an ice-cold penis is a very pragmatic thing, because when Satan had to service the witches who would assemble to draw from his power at the Sabbaths, he could actually remain erect either with those who stimulated him–that is the magician who portrayed Satan–or until he became expended of his sexual vigor. Naturally then, under his fur cloak or garb, he had to strap on something of an artificial nature, a bull's pizzle, a dildo. In the night air, it would cool off. So the witches all swore that the Devil's penis was cold. He would have to use something like this to maintain his position as the Devil.

Fritscher: Then a gay man could service a female witch? Or not...because he'd have the artificial member, but he wouldn't have the real desire.

LaVey: There would be no self-realization.

Fritscher: Witch hunters in their hysteria often see the mark of Satan.

LaVey: It is of interest to me that hippies and Hell's Angels tattoo themselves with the markings of Satanism and other symbols of aggression. Tattooing is an ancient and obscure art. One of the few books on it is called *Pierced Hearts and True Love* by Hanns Ebensten [Britain, 1953]. There's also George Burchet's *Memoirs of a Tattooist* [Britain, 1958]. Certainly much needs to be said of the relation of Satanism and witchery to tattooing. We have members that were tattooed long before the Hell's Angels made it fashionable. One man has the Goat of Bathona, the Satanic Goat, tattooed across his back. Beautifully done. The Devil-headed Eagle is on his chest. Then on each thigh he has the figure of Seth. He's quite spectacular. He has a shaven head and the build of a professional wrestler. He is extremely formidable when he is in ceremony wearing only a black pair of trunks with a very small mask across his eyes. His tattoos are very symmetrically designed attempts at using tattoos for ritualistic purposes.

Fritscher: You paid your dues in burlesque, the circus, and Hollywood. What about witches in popular culture? You were a hit with your "Topless Witches Sabbath" in North Beach.

LaVey: Witchcraft has a lot of show business in it. Religious ritual, after all, was the first theater. For this reason, I think, *Dark Shadows* and *Bewitched* are fine. White witches think these TV shows are terrible because they play the witch as a pretty girl who can snap her fingers and get things done. They try to impress the world that Wicca is not up to that sort of thing. They try to play that they're an intellectually justified "Old Religion." The popular image of the witch is a gal who can get things done in apparently supernatural ways. Like *I Dream of Jeannie.* Why not take advantage of the glamorized witch? If this has been the very element that has brought witchcraft out of a stigmatized, persecuted stereotype, then why put it down? It is the glamorization of witchcraft that gives the erstwhile white witches the free air in which to breathe. Why knock it?

Fritscher: What about these white witches? They back away from the black arts.

LaVey: This gets me to Gerald Gardner, another British type, whom I judge a silly man who was probably very intent on what he was doing. He was motivated to call himself a "hereditary witch" because he had opened a restaurant and needed a gimmick to get it filled with customers. He had taken over a not-too-successful teashop and had turned it into a museum. He had to say he was a research scholar. He got the term *white witch* from a coinage in *Witchcraft's Power in the World Today.* Gardner used the term because witchery was illegal in England at the time. To avoid persecution he opened his museum under the guise of research. He stated he wasn't a witch until the repeal of the laws in 1953. Then he made it very clear he was a "white witch." That's like saying, "Well, I'm a good witch. The others are bad witches. So don't persecute me." Gardner did what he had to do, but I don't think he was any more of an authority on the true meaning of witchcraft than Montague Summers. [Montague Summers, 1880-1948, author of *The Vampire: His Kith and Kin, The Philosophy of Vampirism*, 1928, and *Witchcraft and Black Magic*, 1946.] I think that he simply followed Summers' crappy rituals of circles and "Elohim" and "Adonai." They used the name of "Jesus" and crossed themselves.

Fritscher: Nevertheless, what Gardner dared do in Britain in 1953 for white magic was like the giant step forward you took in the United States in 1966 for black magic.

LaVey: True. I have broken the barrier. I have made it a little bit fashionable to be a black magician. A lot of white witches, however, are still trying to say now that their horned God is not a Devil. It is just a horned God. Well, let me tell you, until five or six years ago they wouldn't even admit to a horned God. Some of them are finally intimating that perhaps they have made pacts with the Devil. For many years the Old Religionists used the writings of Albertus Magnus, the *Sixth and Seventh Books of Moses*, the *Book of Ceremonial Magic*, crossing themselves as they turned the pages, denying theirs was a Christian-based faith.[3] Why in the hell did they use all these Christian accouterments? White witches are no more than a by-product of Christianity, or they wouldn't have to call themselves white witches in the first place. I don't think white witches have the courage of their convictions.

Fritscher: What about Aleister Crowley, the Great Beast, code name "666." How does your demonology doctrine handle this famous Satanist's sex, drugs, and rock-and-roll?

LaVey: I have said that Aleister Crowley had his tongue jammed firmly in his cheek. I think Crowley was a pragmatist. He was also a drug addict [psychedelics and heroin]. The Demons he conjured were the products of a benumbed mind. Basically he was a sweet, kind man who was trying to emancipate himself from the throes of a very strict upbringing. He can't be blamed for anything he did from a

---

3 In the 13th century, writer and bishop, Saint Albertus Magnus (Albert the Great) was the teacher of Saint Thomas Aquinas (1225-1274), the premiere theologian of the Catholic Church. Even during his life, Albertus who died in 1279 was rumored to have been an alchemist who found the "Philosopher's Stone" which according to legend he gave to Thomas Aquinas.

psychoanalytical point of view. He wasn't really that wicked of a man. He had to work overtime at being bad. All the arbitrary numbers, dogma, and so on of his magical curriculum were constructs he invented to answer the needs of his students. Crowley's greatest wisdom was in his *Book of Lies* [1912; followed by *Magick in Theory and Practice*, 1929; and *The Book of the Law*, 1938]. The particular page can be paraphrased: "My disciples came to me, and they asked, 'Oh Master, give us your secret.'" He put them off. They insisted. He said it would cost them ten thousand pounds. They paid, and he gave them his words: "A sucker is born every minute." This one line says more for Crowley than all his other work. His judgment of the popular follower was accurate. Most of the public wants gibberish and nonsense. He alluded to this in his numbering of his *Libers* which are not immense volumes but just a few bound sheets of paper. He's saying the real wisdom is about ten lines long.

Fritscher: Like Crowley and Gardner in Britain, in America, Ray Buckland has done much to spread witchcraft.

LaVey: Ray Buckland. Like Crowley, Gerald Gardner probably knew a good thing when he saw it and got something going that turned out to be more sanctimonious than it should be. Ray Buckland began the same way. Now he admits to being part of the "more mundane" [Wiccan] rather than the "complete esoteric" [Black Magician] he was once made out to be. Ray Buckland certainly knows a great deal about the occult. He has a good synthesis of the Arts. But sanctimony still comes through. His famous chapter on black magic threatens that if a curse is not performed properly it will return to the sender. He defines things like *good* and *bad*, *white* and *black* magic for those who—as I say in my *Satanic Bible*—are frightened by shadows. I maintain that good like evil is only in the eyes of the beholder. Ray Buckland has guts, though, to sit in his Long Island home conducting his rituals and not caring what the neighbors think.

Fritscher: What about Sybil Leek? Another British white witch and astrologer. It's like the British invasion in pop music.

LaVey: I don't know whether Sybil Leek is as big a fool as she sometimes seems, or whether she's laughing up her sleeve. Sybil is a good businesswoman. She helped start the health-food craze and wrote some books. [*The Diary of a Witch* and *The Complete Art of Witchcraft*.] I don't want to judge her. When it comes to white and black magic, she is a good businesswoman. She knows on which side her bread is buttered! My only complaint with Sybil–and I do know her personally–is she has done nothing to dispel all the crap about black and white witches. If she's after the little old ladies in tennis shoes, fine. But she is a dispenser of misinformation.

Fritscher: What about that other Englishman, Alex Sanders, who inherited his white magic tradition from Gerald Gardner.

LaVey: Alex Sanders has become more public in proclaiming himself the "King of the Witches." He is a dispenser of misinformation too. He's not too bad. Actually, in the stifling climate of England he's a forward man among a backward people. He's got a big load. For this I admire him. He's great enough to claim himself King. I don't put as much credence in astrology as he does, because astrology is a case of the tail wagging the dog.

Fritscher: Satan doesn't need the stars?

LaVey: A competent sorcerer, however, should know his astrology because it is a motivating factor for many people. Sydney Omarr, the popular syndicated astrologer, is basically a level-headed guy who sees through a lot of the fraud.

Fritscher: Against the white noise of all these white witches, there you stand: the Black Pope of Black Magic.

LaVey: I'll be the first to give Sybil Leek and Louise Huebner [the official witch of Los Angeles County] and all these people their due. They don't say, "We witches don't want publicity." That takes moxie in a sanctimonious society. They're not like these damn cocktail party witches who can't defend their self-styled reputations when called to do it. These people give me a pain. It's part of being a witch, the ego-gratification of being a witch, to want to talk about it in detail in public.

Afterword

Anton LaVey remains as controversial dead as alive. Although he died on October 29, 1997, his death certificate in the San Francisco coroner's record initially stated that he died October 31, Samhain, Halloween, a few days after he completed his last book, *Satan Speaks*.

Anton LaVey founded the Church of Satan on Walpurgisnacht, April 30, 1966. Thirty-five years later, on Walpurgisnacht, 2001, the eve before May Day, the feast of Beltane, the Church of Satan moved from San Francisco to New York. On October 17, 2001, the owners of 6114 California Street tore down the famous Black House where Anton LaVey founded the Church of Satan. Word got around. On October 31, driving to the annual gay Halloween Party that mobs Castro Street, I stopped and set a bell, a book, and a candle on the curb to mark where once stood the door to the house of a man, who like my longtime friend, the Satanic-Catholic Robert Mapplethorpe, was a cosmic gent.

If in the best books the reader can hear the author's voice, then *The Satanic Bible* is essential LaVey. His work, philosophy, and personality continue, as I understand the connections, with the worldwide Church of Satan under the direction of Magus Peter H. Gilmore, High Priest of the Church and author of *The Satanic Scriptures*. Anton LaVey's surviving companion, Magistra Blanche Barton, who succeeded Diane Hegarty as High Priestess, is the mother of his only son, Satan Xerxes LaVey, and the author of the intimate memoir, *The Secret Life of a Satanist: The Authorized Biography of Anton LaVey*. LaVey has two daughters from two other women: the artist and Buddhist Zeena Schreck, and San Francisco radio-presenter Karla LaVey, founder in 1999 of the First Satanic Church. Magistra Peggy Nadramia, the editor of the horror publication *Grue* magazine, followed Blanche Barton as the current High Priestess of the Church of Satan. She is the wife of Magus Peter H. Gilmore whom she married in 1981.

On its website, the Church of Satan, keeps posted in its canon—with my permission as copyright holder—a monolog version, with my questions deleted, of my interview with the remarkable Anton LaVey.

Visit: www.ChurchofSatan.com

www.ingramcontent.com/pod-product-compliance
Lightning Source LLC
Chambersburg PA
CBHW021200080526
44588CB00008B/432